PERCHED ON NOTHING'S BRANCH

PERCHED
ON
NOTHING'S BRANCH

■ ■ ■

SELECTED POETRY OF
Attila József

TRANSLATED BY PETER HARGITAI

FOREWORD BY MAXINE KUMIN

WHITE PINE PRESS BUFFALO, NEW YORK

WHITE PINE PRESS
P.O. Box 236, Buffalo, New York 14201

Terra Incognita Series: Volume 6
Series Editor: Aleš Debeljak

Selected and translated from the Hungarian: Attila József's Complete Poems
(József Attila Összes Versei, Magvető Kiadó, 1951)

ACKNOWLEDGMENTS: *Apalachee Quarterly:* "Bitter," "Nothing," "Red Lobster";
Blue Unicorn: "Mamma"; *Forum: Ten Poets of the Western Reserve:* "Stones"; *Palmetto
Review:* "A Transparent Lion," "The Bellman of the Lake's Tower," "Drunk on the
Tracks," "Sorrow," "Look"; *Prairie Schooner:* "Weary Man"; *Sands:* "Vision," "Prairie,"
"Culture," "Smoke," "Diamonds"; *Translation Review:* "I Am Not the One Shouting."

This book was published with the support of
the Hungarian Ministry of Culture, the Frankfurt '99 Foundation
and the Chrysopolae Foundation.

Book design: Elaine LaMattina
Printed and bound in the United States of America

LIBRARY OF CONGRESS CATALOGING-IN-PUBLICATION DATA
József, Attila 1905-1937
Perched on nothing's branch : selected poems of Attila József / translated by Peter
Hargitai; introduction by Maxine Kumin.
p. cm.—(Terra incognita ; vol. 6)
ISBN 1-893996-00-X (alk. paper)
1. Title II. Hargitai, Peter
PH3281.J64 A6 1999
894'.51113221–dc21   99-043488
CIP

for Dianne, Suzie and Peter

Contents

The Poems

Preface to the Fifth Edition

I have selected the forty poems in this volume for reasons of chronology as well as organic progression, following Attila József's journey from the adolescent ebullience in his "Strength Song," which he wrote when he was seventeen, through his piercing landscapes of despair and renewal, toward the ultimate disillusionment in one of his last poems, "Nothing," written in the final year of the poet's life.

As a translator, I have allowed myself the freedom to sacrifice, at times, mirror-image fidelity for the sake of creating a better poem in English. And yet, teaching these poems at American universities since their first appearance in 1986, I must admit I was often tempted to revise some of the poems, at times for aesthetic reasons, but then at other times out of a sense of atonement for past infelicities. I am grateful to White Pine Press not only for publishing this fifth edition of *Perched on Nothing's Branch* but also for giving me the long-sought opportunity to revisit these poems with a sharper pen. I should also like to thank my wife, Dianne Kress-Hargitai, for her patient retyping of the current manuscript, and Sanford J. Smoller and László Pethő for their expert proofreading.

And, finally, I am grateful for the kind support of the Hungarian Ministry of Culture and the Frankfurt '99 Foundation in Budapest.

—Peter Hargitai

Foreword

White Pine Press deserves a vote of thanks from all of us. In time for the Frankfurt Book Fair of 1999, which will feature Hungarian poetry, they have reissued the late Attila József's selected poems, *Perched on Nothing's Branch*, in a richly nuanced translation by Peter Hargitai, himself a native-born Hungarian. First published by Apalachee Press of Tallahassee, Florida in 1986, Hargitai's translation won the coveted Landon Translation Prize from the Academy of American Poets in 1988 and promptly went into four editions, a coup for any small press. Now, eleven years later, White Pine Press is continuing to extend the life of this book.

The trajectory of József's life was a sad one. Ghosted by frequent nervous breakdowns, hounded by right wing extremists, at the mercy of a failed love affair, he took his own life in 1937. He was thirty-two years old. Here in the West—and perhaps not only in the West—we have an unfortunate tendency to lionize our suicided poets, as if to take one's own life confers on the work left behind a special grace.

Sylvia Plath, like József, was only thirty-two; Hart Crane, thirty-three; Anne Sexton was forty-five. Berryman was in his fifties when he leapt, waving, off the bridge; Paul Celan, who survived a forced labor camp only to hurl himself into the Seine, fifty. In every instance, tormented by their inner demons, it was, nevertheless, the poetry that kept them alive. Plath, after all, had made a serious earlier attempt to kill herself in her adolescence; Sexton, after an initial postpartum depression, had taken a number of overdoses. Berryman had been unable to conquer his alcoholism, Crane, his frequent bouts of depression. Celan never recovered from the horrors he endured under the Nazi regime.

The general public enjoys a kind of prurient interest in these untimely deaths, perhaps taking them as evidence that poets are moral weaklings, effete creatures unlike themselves, unable to stand up to the pressures of daily life. Yes, we would have been richer had Plath, József and his fellow suicides not succumbed to their separate despairs. The poems they might have written haunt us even today. But let us celebrate what, against enormous odds, they achieved.

We ought also to celebrate poetry itself for sustaining them as long as it did. Certainly for József, poetry provided rich personal rewards, even when he had barely enough money to sustain himself from day to day. All of his poems are cries from the heart, outlets for his supreme though erratic creative drive, his sometimes surreal but surprisingly apt imagery. While *The Columbia Dictionary of Modern European Literature* considers him "the finest Hungarian socialist poet of the 20th century," to contemporary readers he will seem apolitical, more closely associated with the bittersweet lyricism of David Ignatow or John Balaban.

In a startlingly candid curriculum vitae he composed not long before he threw himself under the wheels of a train, Attila József recounts the dry facts of his life. They make fascinating reading and serve as a window as well into history. Communist, socialist, fascist, schizophrenic—despite the designations society provided, the poems never stopped coming. Happily, the vitae is included here and any reader of the poems is advised to begin with József's own account of his life.

Ten months after composing it, in December of 1937, he killed himself. Perhaps it is significant that his adored mother had died at Christmas time. In "Eulogy," one of his most affecting poems, the child's sense of having been willfully abandoned rises to a crescendo of apostrophes:

> I should have eaten you!
> You gave me your own supper—did I ask for it?
> And why did you bend your back to wash clothes?
> So you could straighten it in a wooden box?

Perched on Nothing's Branch contains exactly forty poems, most of them brief, sharp, but invariably built on a scaffolding of arresting images. The poems are ageless, mirroring the human condition and focusing on humankind's existential loneliness.

A searing lyric that addresses József's own mental state but speaks in the voice of our own era declares: "I am not the one shouting; it's the earth rumbling" and then proceeds to offer wild strategies for self-preservation.

slink to the bottom of clear creeks,
cling to crystal,
hide beneath the diamond light
among insects and stones.
Burrow into fresh bread,
you poor dead, you poor dead.
Seep into the earth with showers—
it's useless to bathe in yourself
—wash your face in other faces
as a tiny edge on a blade of grass....

Addressing some of the hazards of translation, Hargitai
has said of the first and last lines of the poem "I Am Not
the One Shouting," that in Hungarian the noun-verb pat-
terns are syntactically parallel, so that literally, the line
translates as: "Not I am shouting, the world is rumbling."
(Moreover, József's original text of this poem is rendered
in capital letters, lest we not hear the intensity of his pitch.)
Hargitai explains that Hungarian, like German, has "an
agglutinative syntax," which means that prepositions, per-
sonal pronouns, and so on get attached to a noun to make
a compound word that may require three or even four
words in English to achieve an intelligible translation.

Utterly contemporary in tone, many of József's poems
ask, as in "Elegy," "Are you also from here? / Where the
longing / never ends to be / like another..." Often, the dic-
tion is flat, deliberately prosaic, then it transmutes into a
burst of imagery. Soapy water has "a little blue head"; "yel-
low trees stand on one foot" is followed by: "That is all I
could write / as I kept falling asleep; / we touched each
other." The voice is melancholy and hauntingly modern.

Train imagery appears in several of József's poems. In

the lyrical "Autumn," "Weariness squats on a boxcar"; in "Look," "The sun's flaming train / rushes past melancholy doorways." In "Winter Night," winter "streaks into the city / on glittering rails." Even a love poem of loss, "Balatonszárszó," contains a train that has already left.

An ambitious poem titled "Consciousness" represents József's bleak, yet gorgeously defiant, credo. "I have seen / blue, red, yellow in dreams / and felt the order of things— / not one stone out of kilter," he tells us. He is hungry for certitude: "Living only on bread /... / Roast beef does not rub / against my mouth...." Despite his searching, "Words lie on one another / like a pile of wood, / squeezing, pressing / each other's being."

The last three stanzas of the poem have been hammered on the anvil for precision. It seems that they presage József's final hours.

> A whole man
> has neither mother nor father in his heart.
> He knows that life
> was given in addition to death,
> and he must give it back
> any moment—like the finder his find.
> He is neither God nor priest.

> But I have seen happiness.
> It was soft and blond and 300 lbs;
> its curly smile wobbled in the pen.
> It lay in a warm puddle,
> squinting, snorting. The light
> was tickling its down.

I live near the tracks.
Trains come and go
with glistening windows.
They are the rush of lighted days.
The poet stands in the wisp of compartments,
leans on his elbows and listens.

Only the satisfied pig can be happy, the poem says, suggesting but not stating the Socratic corollary that it is better to be man dissatisfied. It is only a brief leap to the inner landscape of the poet, who observes "the rush of lighted days,"—the ordinary, illuminated, orderly life that he is shut out of—from his room overlooking the tracks, while standing "in the wisp of compartments." Translator Hargitai defines these wisps as the fleeting flashes of light that come through the compartment windows as the train flies past. Life, József has already told us, is something he must give back at any moment. At some moment, he made the decision to do so.

—Maxine Kumin
Chancellor
Academy of American Poets

PERCHED ON NOTHING'S BRANCH

Curriculum Vitae

I was born in 1905 in Budapest; my religion is Greek Orthodox. My father—the late Áron József—left the country when I was three years old, and through the efforts of the Children's Protective Agency, I was made to live with foster parents at Öcsöd. I lived there until I was seven, already working—as a swineherd—along with the other poor children. When I was seven years old my mother—the late Borbála Pöcze—brought me back to Budapest and enrolled me in the second grade. My mother provided for me and my two sisters by taking on washing and housework. Working at different houses, she was gone from morning till night, and, left without parental supervision, I started skipping school, getting into trouble. It was in a third grade reader that I found some interesting stories about Attila the Hun, so I threw myself into reading. The stories about Attila fascinated me all the more because my name was Attila. My foster parents at Öscöd had insisted on calling me Steve. They said there was no such Christian name as Attila. I was astounded. The very existence of my being was called into question. I believe that it was this experience which made me into a thinking person, one who regards the opinions of others but examines them carefully in his own mind, one who can answer to the name of Steve until it is proven what he had known all along—that his name is Attila.

I was nine when the World War broke out. Our situation worsened. I had to stand in food lines, sometimes from nine in the evening until seven thirty in the morning, only to be told when it got to be my turn that they were out of lard. I helped my mother as best I could. I sold water at the Világ movie theater. I stole coal and firewood from the Ferencváros station to have something to heat with. I made pinwheels from colored paper and sold them to children who were better off. I carried baskets, bags, packages in the shoppers' market, etc. In the summer of 1918, King Károly's Children's Fund sent me on a vacation to Abbázia. My mother was already suffering from a tumor of the uterus, and on my own I asked for assistance from the Children's Protective Agency—and for a brief time they sent me to Monor. Once I was back in Budapest, I sold newspapers, postage stamps, food stamps, blue and white banknotes, like a little banker. During the Rumanian occupation, I worked as a bread boy at the Café Emke. During this time, I was attending secondary school—after five years of elementary.

My mother died in 1919 at Christmas. My brother-in-law, the late Dr. Ödön Makai, was appointed my legal guardian. I spent the spring and summer working on the tugboats *Vihar*, *Török*, and *Tatár* of the Atlantica Shipping Company while preparing for special secondary school examinations as a private student. After this, my guardian and Dr. Sándor Giesswein sent me to a seminary at

Nyergesújfalu so I could begin my training for the Salesian Order. I spent only two weeks there; I am, after all, Greek Orthodox, not Roman Catholic. From here I went to Demke, a boarding school that, after a short time, offered me free tuition. In the summers I earned my room and board by tutoring students around Mezőhegyes. I finished my sixth year of *gymnasium* with honors, despite an attempted suicide probably triggered by adolescence and the problems of transience; then, as before, no one stood by me as a friend. My first poems appeared around this time. I was seventeen when *Nyugat* published some of my poems. They thought I was a child prodigy, when I was just an orphan.

After my sixth year of *gymnasium*, I left the boarding school because I was bored and alone: I had stopped studying and going to lectures, but I still knew my lessons—as my superior grade reports attest. I went to Kiszombor where I did some tutoring and worked in a corn field as watchman and farmhand. On the advice of two kindly teachers of mine, I decided to finish my last two years of study and graduate. As it turned out, I passed all my examinations and graduated a year ahead of my former classmates. I had only three months in which to prepare and that is why I received only a "good" for the seventh grade of *gymnasium* and a "satisfactory" for the eighth. My final examination grades were actually better: I received a grade of satisfactory only in Hungarian and History. It was around this same time that I was accused of blasphemy because of one of my poems. But I was acquitted.

For a time I was a textbook salesman in Budapest, and during the economic inflation, I clerked at the Mauthner private bank. Following the introduction of the Hintz system, I joined the accounting department and soon after, and much to the annoyance of my senior colleagues, I was entrusted with supervising the currency values that were to be paid on account. My enthusiasm started to flag once I was assigned extra duties routinely performed by my senior colleagues, who spent their time jeering at me about my poetry, which was now appearing in periodicals. "I used to write poetry, too, when I was your age," they would laugh. Later, the bank failed.

I made up my mind to be a writer and to find a position closely connected with literature. I registered for courses in Hungarian and French literature and philosophy in the Faculty of Humanities at Szeged University. I attended fifty-two hours of lectures and seminars, but at least now could eat regularly. I was very proud when one of the professors, Lajos Dézsi, nominated me to undertake independent research. My hopes were dashed, however, when another professor, Antal Horger, my examiner in Magyar philology, called me in before two witnesses—I still remember their names; they are teachers now—to make a statement to the effect that I was not to be trusted with the education of the future generation because of the kind of poetry I wrote. Here the professor held up a copy of the periodical where my poem, "Tiszta szívvel" ("With all My Heart"), was published. You talk about the irony of fate. This poem of mine got to be quite famous. Seven articles have been written on the poem since: Lajos Hatvany spoke of it as not only the document of the post-war generation but of "future generations" as well; and writing in *Nyugat* Ignotus said that he "fondled it, caressed it, cherished it in his soul, murmuring, humming" this "wonderful" poem; it was this poem which he placed in his *Ars Poetica* as the model for the new poetry.

The following year—I was twenty then—I went to Vienna, enrolled at the university, sold newspapers in front of the Rathaus-Keller and cleaned the quarters of the Vienna Hungarian Academy. Once Antal Lábán, the director, heard about me, he put an end to all this, provided for meals at the Vienna Hungarian Academy, and found me pupils: I tutored the two sons of Zoltán Hajdu, director of the Anglo-Austrian Bank. From a terrible slum in Vienna, where for four months I had no sheets with which to cover myself, I went straight to the Hatvany castle as guest. The lady of the house, Mrs. Albert Hirsch, gave me traveling expenses to go to Paris at the end of the summer. There I enrolled at the Sorbonne. I spent the next summer in southern France in a fishing village.

After that I returned to Budapest. I completed two semesters at the university. I didn't take my teacher's examinations because—thinking back on Antal Horger's threats—I didn't feel I could secure a position. Once the Foreign Trade Institute was founded, I was hired there to handle French correspondence—my former supervisor, Mr. Sándor Kóródi, will be happy to supply you with a reference. But then I suffered a series of unexpected setbacks that—no matter how life had touched me—made it unbearable for me to go on. The OTI Health Service referred me to a sanatorium for neurasthenia. I resigned my job to avoid being a burden on the young institute. I live now solely from my writing. I am editor of *Szép szó*, a literary and critical periodical. Other than my native Hungarian, I write and read French and German, can write Hungarian and French business correspondence, and consider myself a good typist. I used to know shorthand—all I need is a month's practice. I am familiar with printing techniques, I can express myself clearly. I consider myself honest and, I believe, perceptive, and when it comes to work, I am sturdy by nature.

Note: József wrote this as part of a job application in February, 1937, ten months before he committed suicide.

The Poems

Strength Song

Seventeen-year muscles ripple across my back.
My eye does not dim at the edge of the horizon.
I toss spring over my shoulder
and bring it to my heart.
I bear the yoke of my untimeliness:
knees under heavier sighs do not bend.
I hoard the flaming dragon of the ages,
the tongue that wrings the page's sorrow.
Pyramid worlds crumble under my feet,
my head butts heaven, the sun crowns me,
all the wounds drain from my clenched fists
and I can still kneel humbly
over the rough grass of my mother's grave.

With All My Heart

I have no father and no mother,
I have no God, I have no land,
neither cradle, nor a cover,
nor kiss, nor lover's hand.

Three days I haven't eaten
not too much and not too well,
all I have is twenty years,
twenty years I'll gladly sell.

If no one takes them,
maybe then the devil will.
I'll break in with all my heart,
and if need be, kill.

They'll catch me, they'll hang me,
cover me up with blessed earth,
and death-eating grass will start
growing on my lovely heart.

Bethlehem

Soft crows sit on cotton clouds,
twilight droops between branches.
Two staff-bearing shepherds and three kings
tilt against the beaten floor.
A woman descends the ladder—
"Angels from on high," five elders sing.
Outside the window an old man
pitches manure to clucking chickens.
Muddy potatoes cower in hay needles.
The thatch roof bristles, holy soup ascends
toward the ceiling.
Jesus, in a playpen of yellow down,
is mirthful among the paper sheep.
By firelight men of good will
make hay around the manger.
The lordly wind drives the common straw,
two shepherds munch on gingerbread,
three kings guzzle their liquor.

Red Lobster

Shadows of silverfish sweep the corals,
usher in the blackness, flutter on soft sand;
they touch tired snails and fall asleep for
       a long time;
I watch the man-of-war's transparent light
and weed a path with rugged scissors,
sending ripples upward in clean water—

Where the sheen is most brilliant,
come there.
In my many strivings
I offer an ineffectual ray to the light;
think of me too and keep vigil
in your garden where the shells blossom
with open wings.

Strong currrents harden my armor,
and only you can understand its redness—
a blue sea urchin shines on my back;
I wait for you by the whitest stone.

The waves rush quickly from the hill.
The lobster sends fat morsels
toward the urchin's fluttering petals.

Weary Man

Over the fields somber peasants start
silently home.
We lie next to each other, the river and I,
limp grass sleeps beneath my heart.

The river is quiet, ushers great peace,
all my troubles dissolve into vapor;
I am neither Magyar, child, nor brother—
only the weary lie here.

Night passes out the silence,
I am a piece of its warm bread,
heaven sleeps now, and the stars
rest on my forehead
and on the quiet Maros.

Autumn

Autumn fog is scraping
bald interlacing branches,
frost squints on the railing.

Weariness squats on a boxcar,
dreaming of the steam engine
as it winds home on the tracks.

A few despondent yellow hills
disrobe and whine.
Damp adhesions flounder on the stone.

Blushing summer packed away
her rags, rushing off
as unexpectedly as she came.

Autumn was already lurking
about the yard, drooling
between the bricks.

I knew she would come,
and I'd have to heat the room.
I couldn't believe she would be here
so soon, looking into my eyes,
whispering into my ear.

Eulogy

I burn with a fever of ninety-eight point six
        and, mother, you won't even nurse me.
Like a loose girl you stretch
beside the angel of death.
I try to piece you together
from autumn scenes and a lot of women
but there's not enough time.
        The fire consumes me.

The last time I went to Szabadszállás
        it was the end of the war
and Budapest was in shambles,
without bread.
I lay flat on a boxcar,
bringing you potatoes, chicken, a sack of millet,
        but you weren't there.

You took it from me and gave yourself
        and your breast to the worms.
You used to comfort and scold me
but I see now your words were all lies.
You warmed my soup, blew it, and stirred it,
and said: eat and grow tall, my love.
Now your lips taste only the dampness—
        you lied to me on purpose!

I should have eaten you!
You gave me your own supper—did I ask for it?
And why did you bend your back to wash clothes?
So you could straighten it in a wooden box?

Look, I'd be happy if you could beat me once more!
You would make me happy because I would strike back:
You're terrible! You strive not to be,
        you ruin everything, you shadow!

You're more of a cheat than any woman
who whores and tells lies!
You secretly gave up on love
and the living faith you had painfully borne.
You're a gypsy! What you have given with love
you stole back in the last hour!
I feel like cursing—
Mamma, can't you hear? Yell at me!

It's over. My head slowly clears.
The child who hangs on his mother
discovers how foolish he is;
anyone born is cheated in the end
so he might as well cheat or cry.
Either way he will die.

I Am Not the One Shouting

I'M NOT THE ONE SHOUTING, IT'S THE EARTH
    RUMBLING.
LOOK OUT, LOOK OUT, SATAN'S GONE CRAZY,
SLINK TO THE BOTTOM OF CLEAR CREEKS,
CLING TO CRYSTAL,
HIDE BENEATH THE DIAMOND LIGHT
AMONG INSECTS AND STONES.
BURROW INTO FRESH BREAD,
YOU POOR DEAD, YOU POOR DEAD.
SEEP INTO THE EARTH WITH SHOWERS—
IT'S USELESS TO BATHE IN YOURSELF
—WASH YOUR FACE IN OTHER FACES
AS A TINY EDGE ON A BLADE OF GRASS AND
YOU'LL BE GREATER THAN THE WORLD'S AXIS.

OH, MACHINES, BIRDS, BLOSSOMS, STARS!
A BARREN MOTHER TREMBLES FOR BIRTH.
MY FRIEND, MY DEAR LOVING FRIEND,
HOWEVER TERRIBLE, HOWEVER GRAND,
I'M NOT THE ONE SHOUTING, IT'S THE EARTH
    RUMBLING.

Winter Night

Be disciplined!
Summer's sheen
is gone.
Embers flicker
above charred heaps.
The country is quiet,
the air's
fine glass
is scratched by thickets.
Lovely humanity. Only a thin strip
of silver cloth—some kind of ribbon—
hangs desperately on
a branch.
The only smile
on these knotty boughs.

In the distance
gnarled mountains like heavy hands
hold the dying light,
the smoking village,
the flaccid moss,
the round silence of the valleys.

A peasant plods home to his hovel.
Joints stare blankly at the soil.
A cracked hoe hobbles on his shoulder;
the handle bleeds, the iron bleeds.
The heavy hands, the heavy shovel
trudge out of existence.

Night ascends with sparkling stars
like smoke from a chimney.

A church bell
rolls in the steel-blue night,
and the heart is still, and something else,
the living land
beats on, the winter night, the winter sky, the
winter ore
is the bell
and its tongue is the earth, the forged and
heavy earth,
and the heart is the voice.

The intellect weighs the memory of chimes:
winter struck its anvil and ironed
a border of sky.
Wheat, light, hay
pour down
all summer long.

They glitter
like the soul of thought
this winter night.

Silence locks the world
by forging a moon.

A raven wafts through frigid space
and the lull cools.
Bone, can you hear the lull?
The clinking of the molecules?

What cabinet can hold
such sparkling nights?

A branch lifts a dagger to the frost,
the black void trembles,
crows float up and down
in the fog.

Winter night.

A freight train comes
like a separate darkness,
smoke stars swirl and die
in infinite slices.

The light darts across boxcars
like a mouse.
The flame of this winter night.

Winter steams
above cities,
streaks into the city
on glittering rails. Blue frost.
Yellow light's flame.

It makes sharp weapons of anguish
in the city,
this relentless night.

On the outskirts
streetlights fall like sodden hay.

A coat rustles,
a man is hunkering down,
winter has stomped on his foot...

As rusty branches lean
out of the fog
he embraces this winter night
as his own.

Monument On A Mountaintop

for Endre Ady

This is a glass mountain.
Devils slide up and down its slopes.
This mound was built long ago with the rinds
of ruined souls. And at midnight the mountain sings
to the dark world.

Hi-lee-ho, he died! ... Oh, he died! ... Long
silence,
the mountain flames, starts to dance,
something grave climbs to the top and stops,
high up there it stops. Lies down. A pale
spirit falls tepidly from its face.

The mountain crystallizes into stairs.
You can see far from the top
and even farther from the shrine:
who wants to look?
Only silence. And the mountain roars, shines.

Insects

We creep forward
as marvelous insects.
Were we clouds we would come
only in drought,
avoid picnickers
gathering litter lest
it rain tomorrow.
Our threadbare bodies
heat up in summer.
Insects play a week in a day.
From a hidden bush
birds watch their mating.

A pebble is innocent,
unearthed in the scented
footprints of these girls.
It cannot be me or the grass,
though I am friend to everything:
the hazelnut gratefully splits
in my hand. A branch brushes
a straw left tangled in my hair.
Meadow after meadow is like the arms
of a woman who leads young men
with the spread of her skirt.
They fan her fragrance
and blossom with bald marvelous shields
turned toward the sun.

Paris

A patron never rises in the morning.
In Paris Jeanettes are Berthas and
a man can buy cooked spinach
or burning candles at the barbershop.

Sixty naked women sing to heaven
all the way down the St. Michel
and Notre Dame: it's cold inside,
and for five francs you can see me
from above.

The Eiffel tower tilts during the night
and nestles under quilted fog,
a policeman will kiss you if you're a girl
and there are no seats on the toilets.

Glassmakers

Glassmakers start great fires,
and in their kettles mix sweat
and blood with matter until limpid.
They are poured into tablets,
the last drop of their strong hands
roll them smooth until perfect.

As the sun dawns over cities
and village hovels, they spread
the light. Sometimes we call them
hired hands, sometimes poets,
though there is little distinction.
Slowly they bleed all color
and become transparent, brilliant,
great crystal windows through which
they can see what is to come.

Smoke

A smoke wisp blossoms in front of the moon,
silver sashes tie, unbind, and bow.
Cool air seeps through the cloud.

I have suffered till I'm worn.
I fly off like common day troubles—
cool air seeps through the cloud.

I fly off, but then a feverish tremor
for life rocks the world and
seeps through the cool air.

Bitter

O radioactivity! I'm reading, eating a watermelon
        and I know
        the world changes only within us.
I'm only a colored rattle, do you hear me? My face
        is transparent, behind it flowers soar,
popped from electronic waves.
A humanist century tears me from my love, oh flicked-off
        sorrow. Burn the orphanages.
Lambs are sheep, and I'm an ass,
        not even the shadow of a shepherd.
If I close my eyes airplanes crash, and those too
        that wing from me daily.
Glittering dust, halt your gilded motors because
        she will sweep you out in the morning.
O woman, my lover's tears can drive
        those ancient turbines
and it's a shame,
but let this whistling apprentice grinder live.
He doesn't even know the sky
has sailed into his wallet.

Vision

The eagle
swoops down cliffs.
Lightning with wings,
conceived out of nothing.
More than abiding,

its brilliant blue beak
swallows everything;
steel claws tear
warm meat

and the crying.
Bloody down glistens,
eyes paint
the dawn red.

What eagle! What thought!
What shadow it carves,
the night, delight, love
into the sparking stars.

A wing is song,
the other, Flora,
charging the night's
lightning.

Night on the City's Edge

The night slowly lifts
its net from the yard;
the kitchen fills with mist
like the bottom of a pond.

Silence—the scrub brush
rises to its feet and crawls.
Above it a piece of wall
ponders whether to drop.

Everything sighs
in oily rags,
sits on the city's edge,
then walks across the square
to ignite a feeble moon.

Mills loom
like ruins
to conceive
a denser dark,
the pedestal of silence.

Through the windows
the moon floats
in sheaves,
threads each chair
with light
until morning.

As the work stands still
the power loom spins
the weaver's crumbling dreams.

Steel yards,
cement yards, tool and die,
like graveyards. Mausoleums
guard the secret of resurrection:
a cat scrapes the fence,
the night watchman sees a ghost—
dynamos glitter
like fireflies.

Trains whistle.

Dampness gropes in the twilight
and curdles the dust
among the leaves.

A policeman.
Someone with leaflets
crosses the street
on catpaws, sniffs
the pavement like a dog
and avoids the streetlamp.

The tavern's window
vomits sour light into pools.
The choking light flickers,
only a hired hand keeps vigil.
The bartender snores, hisses,
bares his teeth at the wall,
then runs up syphillitic steps

and cries. Cries for revolution.

Taut waters lash
into cooled steel.
The wind howls, laps
it with a dog's tongue.

Sacks of hay like barges
float silently on the edge of night—

the warehouse is a bottomless ship,
the foundry's ore boat conceives,
red seeds spark into form.

Everything is damp. Everything heavy.
Mildew traces squalid maps
on bare fields
where the grass is in rags. A piece of paper
stirs but is powerless to move...

Damp, clinging wind.
The flapping of dirty sheets,
oh night!
You hang in the air like frayed calico,
on the line like dredged sorrow.
Poor man's night! Coal,
smolder my heart,
melt steel
for an anvil that can't break,
a hammer pounds, a blade, the edge
of victory, oh night!

The night is somber, the night is heavy.
I am also asleep, my brothers.
Don't let torment twist our souls
or the worm prick our tender bodies.

Sorrow

I came out here into the forest.
The leaves rustle like handbills,
the silence of the earth

lies dully, arms and limbs reaching out
for power...a dry branch
falls on my head.

It hurts only for a moment,
almost gnashing,
not only for a moment, just

that a rabid dog attacked me
and I came out to gather
what strength I had left.
Like an old woman, the sorrow.

Teardrops? An ant drank of it
and saw his face.
It will not work anymore.

Consciousness

I.
Dawn sifts earth from sky
and at her soft cry
all the insects and children
swirl into sunlight;
not a drop of dampness,
only brilliant light!
Last night the leaves lit
the trees like tiny butterflies.

II.
I have seen
blue, red, yellow in dreams
and felt the order of things—
not one stone out of kilter.
Muted light seeps into joints,
dreams and steel become the one
and only order. The moon rises
by day, and by night, the sun.

III.
Living only on bread
I reach for something
more certain than dice
among the idle and the frivolous.
Roast beef does not rub
against my mouth or a child
against my heart. Lips,
however clever, cannot catch them,
nor the cat the mouse

both inside and out.

IV.
Worlds lie on one another
like a pile of wood,
squeezing, pressing
each other's being.
What-cannot-be always
sprouts branches,
what-will-be are the flowers,
what-is smashes into pieces.

V.
Like a stump of silence
I tilt against the wood
in the freightyard;
grey weed touches my mouth,
raw, oddly sweet.
Still as a corpse. I follow
the watchman's moods,
his shadow flickers
on wet coal in the boxcar.

VI.
The torment inside
cries out for redemption.
The earth is a wound that festers
and singes, and the fever is the soul,
a slave of rebellion—
free only when we build a house
where the landlord has no dominion.

VII.
I looked beyond the night
at the cog-wheel of heaven and saw
in the smog of my dream
threads of braided cables
out of which the loom
of the past weaves its law
only to burst at the seams.

VIII.
Silence cocks its ear. Strikes one.
We may still reclaim our youth,
imagine a little freedom
between prison walls—the stars
in the Milky Way are shining bars.

IX.

I heard the thunder of iron.
I heard the laughter of rain.
I saw the past rent asunder,
forgetting mere images.
Broken under all this weight
all we can do is love—
lest we forge weapons of rage.

Consciousness.

X.
A whole man
has neither mother nor father in his heart.
He knows that life
was given in addition to death,
and he must give it back
any moment—like the finder his find.
He is neither God nor priest.

XI.
But I have seen happiness.
It was soft and blond and 300 pounds;
its curly smile wobbled in the pen.
It lay in a warm puddle,
squinting, snorting. The light
was tickling its down.

XII.
I live near the tracks.
Trains come and go
with glistening windows.
They are the rush of lighted days.
The poet stands in the wisp of compartments,
leans on his elbows and listens.

Elegy

Under bloated leaden skies
smoke floats above the landscape,
as my soul, hovering low,
too heavy to soar.

Hardened spirit, delicate images,
follow the truth of the ages,
footprints toward the self,
toward the source. Look below

to another time
when you squatted under
tumultuous skies
by haggard bulkheads
by the silence of anguish,
foreboding, pleading,
dissolving the thickness
of gloom in the mingling
of millions.

A whole race
is molded here. Everything in ruins.
The stiff dandelion opens its parasol
in the blight of foundry yards.
Through broken shards
the day ascends its sallow stairs
in sodden light.

Answer me.
Are you also from here?

Where the fierce longing
to be like another wretched sage
never ends, squeezed
by this enormous age,
the visage distorted in every line?

Rest here. Where crippled borders
creak and groan,
keep vigil over a priggish order.
Recognize yourself? We wait here
for a future that is planned, solid, lovely
as plots dreaming tall houses
weaving the noise of life. Only shards
wedged in mudcracks can look at the grass
with those marble eyes.

A thimbleful of sand
is sprayed from the dunes. Drone.
Green and black flies swirl
for man's scraps and the rag. A table
is set on a mortgaged plot of blessed
mother earth. Yellow grass
blooms in iron spittoons.

You know it.
That desolate joy
that yanks you back and forth
to a landscape that won't
let you go? The exquisite
suffering that keeps you here?
Children beaten
into faraway corners

longing for their mothers.
Where you can
at last cry and smile,
where you can bear
to be yourself,
oh my soul! This is my home.

Mamma

For a week, stopping now and then,
I think only of mamma.
Carrying a creaking laundry basket,
she briskly went up to the attic.

And I was such a bold little man,
I screamed and raved and stamped my feet:
Leave those damp clothes to someone else,
take me up to the attic.

She went on and hung the clothes mutely,
she didn't scold, she didn't look at me,
and the clothes glistened, whispering,
dangling high in the wind.

I wouldn't whimper, but it's too late,
I see now how enormous she is;
her gray hair flows into heaven,
she blues the waters of the sky.

Balatonszárszó

1.
Autumn howls,
rips green into foam.
Small storms play hide and seek,
flies are dying by the window.

The landscape whirls and delights
in the bright spaces of silence.
Yellow trees stand on one foot
and blink at the sun.

Snatched into the current
I long for a bed.
I have packed away my homespun
clothing and dress somberly
in finer linen.

2.
The night reels in large irritable waves;
water gurgles underneath the boat, yet
I find a lovely melancholy mood in your lap.

Autumn is cold.
People are always sad when they learn
to tremble again. Cool shadows start
the old ones coughing.

3.
Je n'ai point de thème,
excepté que je t'aime—
That is all I could write
as I kept falling asleep;
we touched each other.

She wore glasses on her nose
and looked at me from under them.

I pressed her to me and she closed her eyes
under her glasses. We were always disturbed.

The train left.

But I didn't linger for long;
it rained and I went home.

She left me a hundred grams of tobacco
for cigarettes.

No dreams, only sleep.
We will not see each other again.

A Transparent Lion

A transparent lion lives between black walls,
I wear a pressed suit in my heart when I speak to you,
I mustn't think of you before my work is done,
you're dancing,
I haven't had any bread and will live a long life,
it's been five weeks, I don't know where you are,
time runs off on wooden legs
and the streets are buried by the snow;
I wonder if anyone could love you.
Mute Negroes play chess for your long silences.

Angry for You

When the sun comes up
the dew dries on the hairs
of those who never rage.
My anger will never hurt you.

I am in this spacious field
where I may fall. Aging mastmakers
come in swelling lines
with their masts
and, winning there,
six million
steelworkers heave clanging
hammers at the sky. Into
the heavenly storm of tools,
I take your kisses with me there.

You don't even notice
how I puff myself up when I speak
of the future. If you wish
I will return after the triumph
of the singing cities:
the bakers will tie their breadboards
together and carry me pompously
with floury heads
to your bed.

My anger will never hurt you.
Take the hand that holds you high
over the rage of his dreams.

Soapy Water

Huddled between bricks
in the chilly courtyard,
cautiously dissolving
into nooks and crannies,

soapy water surges forward, stops.
Here and there its little blue head,
its almost invisible
feeler trembles

as it surveys each obstacle.
Like a captive it runs about
till death overtakes it
and passes it by.

The twitching skin
shakes its foamy mane. Yellow light
glows on a blue-green body

night's ashen fingers can't find.
It will not be. But as it trembles,
its slight shiver passes through me—

the intrusion of thought.

I would fly. And this branch would fly.
The house. The hay. The cloud.
All things linking this world.

The Smoke

Factory smoke
spirals toward heaven,
silver sparks braid
ashes in air.

She kneads clenched fingers,
steals away the sorrow and the tears.
The sorrow and the tears.
But if it pleases her
she can burn and kill.

She falls upon the wailing wall,
shrouds an arm

and offering a valiant prayer
in her darkness, in her pride
she ascends almost to God
somewhere.

Stones

Don't be angry with me, ancient stones,
because I trample you. I'm much better
at the art of trampling than you.

I'm talking to you, old brothers.
Something heavier tramples me under,
walking on headstones, on silent haunches,
it doesn't speak, except through omens:
O mute ones, is it you?
Are these your heavy words
I can't understand?

Why are there stones and no buildings?

Doesn't prayer or hallelujah help?
Or faith? or mortar, for Christ's sake?
We fell, scattered into a million pieces
like adobe in the rain.
Where's the strong, rock-solid man
who knows of no pain?
It's unbearable like this,
lying in the street,
and no one will build us into cities
or granite mountains, though when young
we were lapping hills
where peace and brotherhood lived.

Insolence and bombs broke us apart.
Sunk into geyser-footed blood,
a hundred succoring brains smolder
like lime

that we may grow into sunlit cities.
Because our only concern now
are the stones lying in the street,
trampled in the mire and dust,
longing to be a temple's towering dome!

Medallions

1.
I was an elephant, pious and pure
drank of waters wise and cool,
stood on a hill and with my trunk
caressed the moon and the sun,

and I lifted to their faces
flint, trees, snakes, dung beetles,
and now my soul: heaven disappears.
I fan myself with monstrous ears.

2.
Dust crawls on dew drops,
hands hide holes in overalls,
the swineherd sobs, strokes
a piglet charmed into stone—

slow to blush, the sky smokes greenly,
chimes ripple over the dull lagoon;
frozen into sheets is the milk-white flower
on whose falling leaf hangs the world—

3.
The leech-fisher shambles, shambles,
the bony swineherd marvels, marvels,
herons hover, hover over the pools,
fresh cowpie steams, cools—
a tired apple hangs over my head,

chewed to the core for a worm's eye view
through which some can see the world,
the poem as an apple blossom, a flower—

4.
You ought to be milkfoam,
a murmur in the still night,
maybe a knife under rusty water,
maybe a loose button rolling—

a servant girl's tears fall into dough;
don't look for kisses when
there's a fire in the house,
pick up your feet, find your way home—
smoldering eyes will light the way—

5.
A pig with knuckles of jasper
sits on a god carved from alabaster.
Hey, velvet shroud, thou art milkfoam.
I will die a bard with a massive beard.

And if my heavenly skin cramps into folds,
the fat of my stomach curdles into rolls
to swarm like white maggots,
to glisten like so many stars.

6.
It's my fate
the green lizard seeks.
Wheat rustles, casts out seeds;
a stone drops, the lake takes me in.

The lake, the sky, and the grave.
War prophesying dawns
reel around my nodding head,
fleeting days and trembling stars
feverish with the world's dead.

7.
On the threshold is a steel-wool bucket—
love the girl who sweeps barefooted.
Dirty water evaporates,
the scum dries where
she rolled up her sleeves—

I am warping into tin bubbles.
Free and ringing they burst
over water like sea horses
over the glittering teeth of staircases—

8.
A lawyer petrifies into amber,
squats, stares in black tails,
probes his envious cover, pets, blesses
the light, the wind, the haze—

A rose runs in here as I rot,
cool herons pick my flesh to flakes,
I become the oozing warmth of autumn nights
lest old men break out in gooseflesh—

9.
I share a solitary bed with a friend.
There will be no lily withering.
I have no Gatling gun, stone, or arrow,
though I'd like to kill like anyone else.

And the beans simmer and hiss.
Your sauce-colored eyes see
my blathering jowls rolling in a fever
as swallows keep feeding me insects—

10.
Curl up, my beard, crackle, sizzle,
fork and harrow the fields—
above the sky, below the clouds
where an unclaimed caress is still afloat,

till its cool magic is brought to rest
in my beard whose red rivulets
trickle from the steam of good vintage.

11.
Twenty-three kings
wear crowns of jasper
and eat honeydew melons.
A new moon shines in their left hand.

Twenty-three young men swagger,
wear clumsy hats
and slurp watermelon.
A new sun shines in their right hand.

12.
The black one has a flattened nose,
the yellow a halo of a bluer sky,
the redman's skin is burnt the most,
the white man is a flailing ghost—

I Threw It

I threw myself here while the blind knocked about
our hearts. Our intentions are one with radium,
tomorrow we will be Jehovahs making ourselves anew.
Yes, this is love and the song of the river-lyre
whose chords we stretch till the water washes
her ankles. A wavelength measures my height,
and I call the giddy solar system "kisses"—
prayers smiling under sonorous black tresses.
Hours wither into oppressive dreams
but a violet garden swims inches above cities,
a train runs toward them and a slim tower
cries to them in the shadow of tears.
Think of lyres in the eyes of young poets
with no one to wash them in life-giving water.

On Glasses

Glasses are fresh clean plants:
they glitter, dew cleaves to them;
should we stare at them long enough
they will ring out softly.

Glasses bloom in the hearts of springs
but the glassmakers are ignorant
of their secret.
Men and women keep mistaking
each other's glasses.

I had mixed them up myself once
and since then no glass of water
has been sweet enough,
though a bird dying of thirst will
notice the many shiny glasses
beyond the clouds.

Everything Is Old

Everything is old here. The ancient storm
leans on lightning's crooked shoulder
and whistles at the thorn-whiskered rose.
They hobble on bad feet.

Everything is old. The revolution
squats, coughing on sharp
scattered stones, a coin shines
in his bony hand: my favorite song.

Why isn't my hand transparent-old,
so that, touching a wrinkle on my face,
it would fall into my lap. Seeing
they would believe: tears roll from my eyes.

O my youth. My saintly age.
Flailing cool fish
swarm in the net of red dusk
and frogspawn curdles the dust
of my dying wish.

Diamonds

Psalms are forever.

We stand on a diamond mountain,
our pockets full of pebbles.
And forgetting we were angels,
we stuffed our wings into fat quilts.
Entreaties only cry for our strength
and stones have worn holes under our knees,
stars frozen in each breast.

Yes. Yes.
The sailors have foundered.
Meek oarsmen paddle toward God,
even the old ones
who sit on the simple wharf
and preach patience
to the ephemeral fish.

Yes. Yes.
Let's not forget, my friends,
we row with our fists instead of oars!
Everything has to be stroked lovingly,
the frogs as well as the wolves.

We stand on a diamond mountain,
harsh snow, cover our trespasses,
heavenly gossamer, loosen our tongues
into—oh—infinite crystals!

Rain

it rains rains
dust curdles on bodies

thunder-ring
can you hear them pounding
on our hearts?

naked
to run to run
toward the forest with open arms

rain rain
you hold out your tiny finger
for the blasting ring

the wind had brought it
the wind
from laughing girls
who let their hair down long

over the dry leaves
heartlessly
through the spaces between the trees

Drunk on the Tracks

A drunk is lying on the tracks,
he clutches a flask in his left hand
and snores as if in the arms of his lover.
The night has frittered away the day.

The wind tousles weeds and litter
into his hair, wraps him in godly mist
so he doesn't stir, except for a chest
that heaves strangely.

Like a rail-tie, the hardness of his fist;
he can sleep there as on his mother's lap.
His clothes are rags. He is young. A man.

There's no room for the sun, the sky is ashes.
Only a drunk is lying on the tracks,
and from far away, the slow boom of the earth.

Yellow Grass

Yellow grass spears through the sand,
bony old woman, this wind:
the puddle is a strange brute,
the sea calm, willing to chat.

I hum my silent inventory:
a home that might as well be
a coat for sale,
dusk dissolving into dunes—
I have no words to go on.

Time glistens its coral reef:
grass, trees, timber,
house, woman swarm into
harried currents of sky.

Look

The sun's flaming train
rushes past melancholy doorways.

Go, your footprints
no longer hurt.

Silence.
Only a splash,
I give back my fat fish to the river,
a whisper,
I give back my frail bird to the field.
Just go.
The flower hides
withering leaves.

Look,
night
falls.

The Bellman of the Lake's Tower

Just like a man who's broke
I mixed beet-leaves in with my tobacco
for which my pipe thanked me
as it sucked in, coughed,
and looked after its blue
son of a smoke,
who got as far as the lake's tower
where soulful violas, still cloudy,
composed and resolved themselves
into poetry:
it was about virgin boys and the lake,
and hairs of gold.
Wake up and look how tall you've grown—
why even the man at the store says
your mother will be buying you
long pants
soon.
And there
in the tower,
despite the prohibition against alcohol,
the bellman who hanged himself
is dangling in his long pants.

Perched on Nothing's Branch

I finally arrive
at the sand's wet edge,
look around, shrug

that I am where I am,
looking at the end. A
silver ax strokes
summer leaves. Playfully.

I am perched solidly
on nothing's branch.
The small body shivers
to receive heaven.

Iron-colored.

Cool shiny dynamos revolve
in the quiet revolution of stars.
Words barely spark from clenched teeth.

The past tumbles
stonelike through space,
blue time floating off
without a sound. A blade
flashes, my hair—

My mustache is a full
caterpillar drooping
down my numb mouth,
my heart aches, words are cold.
There's no one out here
to hear—

Dew

A raspberry bush squats,
cradles the greasy paper
slumbering in her arms.

The earth is soft, the night
delicate as a pearl.
Thick, twisting branches
braid softly. Mountain mists
tremble to my song.

I have worked all day
humming like the fields.
How easy heaven can be!
My workshop is dark now.

I am tired or simply good.
I shimmer like the grass.
Like the stars.

Nothing

Nothing, nothing, nothing, nothing, nothing.
Let it be, so it won't be,
let it be, so it won't be—let us say: Edith.
Small invisible yellow chickens
peck at the stars.

Maybe it's dawn and Budapest is burning.
Maybe it's the paint that melts
on a giant girl's sweltering face.

Cars rumble, shutters rattle,
the sea thunders, people swarm.

That rude house on the corner makes me angry—
it's like scurf on a child's face.

Or is this an unfamiliar morning,
            or a foreign railway station
where I've come?

I have no luggage.
There's something I forgot—maybe if I remember.
One: nothing.
Two: nothing.
Three: nothing.
Sounds peculiar as the rail station
where there's nothing at all.

Attila József: A Chronology

1905   Born in Budapest on April 11.

1908   József's father abandons family.

1910   József is sent to the small village of Öcsöd to live with foster parents.

1912   His mother brings him back to Budapest.

1919   His mother dies and his brother-in-law is appointed guardian.

1922   József publishes his first book of poetry, A szépség koldusa (Beauty's Beggar), while still in secondary school.

1924   Enters the University of Szeged.

1925   Leaves the university without attaining a degree after a clash with a professor over his poem, "Tiszta szívvel," (With All My Heart). His second volume of poetry, Nem én kiáltok (I Am Not the One Shouting), is published.

1926   Goes to Vienna where he lives by selling newspapers and cleaning rooms. After a few months, he moves to Paris where he reads Hegel and Marx.

1927   He returns to Hungary and, after an unhappy
        love affair, has his first nervous breakdown.
        Becomes active in the socialist movement.

1928   First hospitalization for neurasthenia.

1930   He joins the Communist Party.

1931   His revolutionary volume, *Döntsd a tőkét!* (Chop
        at the Root [or] Knock Down the Capital), is pub-
        lished and is seized by the public prosecutor.
        Begins psychoanalytic treatment.

1932   *Külvárosi éj* (Night in the City) is published.

1933   Labeling him a fascist, the Communist Party severs
        its association with József.

1934   His sixth volume, *Medvetánc* (Bear Dance) is pub-
        lished.

1936   *Nagyon fáj* (It Hurts Deeply) is published. His last
        three books are praised, and in 1936, he becomes
        editor of the left-wing literary review *Szép szó.*
        However, his mental health begins to rapidly
        deteriorate. Schizophrenic episodes become more
        frequent.

1937   In December he commits suicide by throwing
        himself under a train.

A Note on the Translator

American poet Peter Hargitai is a free translator in the tradition of Ezra Pound's translations from the Chinese and György Faludy's translations of Villon. He was born in Budapest, Hungary, and he emigrated to the United States after the Hungarian Revolution of 1956.

He has taught English at numerous universities including the College of the Bahamas, the University of Miami, the University of Massachusetts, and Florida International University where he is currently on the English faculty.

He is the winner of the Landon Translation Award from the Academy of American Poets, a Fulbright Fellowship, a Florida Arts Council Fellowship, and the Füst Milán Award from the Hungarian Academy of Arts and Sciences.